ARACHNID WORLD

HARVESTMEN

SANDRA MARKLE

SECRET
OPERATIVES

◣ LERNER PUBLICATIONS COMPANY MINNEAPOLIS

FOR CURIOUS KIDS EVERYWHERE

ACKNOWLEDGMENTS

The author would like to thank Dr. James C. Cokendolpher, Museum of Texas Tech University; Dr. Tom Eisner, Cornell University; Dr. Simon Pollard, Canterbury Museum, Christchurch, New Zealand; Dr. William Shear, Hampden-Sydney College, Hampden-Sydney, Virginia; and Joe Warfel, Eighth-Eye Photography, Arlington, Massachusetts, for sharing their expertise and enthusiasm. A special thanks to Skip Jeffery for his support during the creation of this book.

Lerner Publications Company
A division of Lerner Publishing Group, Inc.
241 First Avenue North
Minneapolis, MN 55401 U.S.A.

Website address: www.lernerbooks.com

Library of Congress Cataloging-in-Publication Data

Markle, Sandra.
    Harvestmen : secret operatives / by Sandra Markle.
      p.   cm. — (Arachnid world)
    Includes bibliographical references and index.
    ISBN 978-0-7613-5042-2 (lib. bdg. : alk. paper)
    1. Opiliones—Juvenile literature. I. Title.
  QL458.5.M37 2011
  595.4'3—dc22   10/11   2010023491

Manufactured in the United States of America
1 - DP - 12/31/10

CONTENTS

AN ARACHNID'S WORLD

WELCOME TO THE WORLD OF ARACHNIDS

(ah-RACK-nidz). Arachnids can be found everywhere on Earth
except in the deep ocean.

So how can you tell if an animal is an arachnid rather
than a relative like a centipede *(below)*? Both arachnids and
centipedes belong to a group of animals called arthropods
(AR-throh-podz). The animals in this
group share some traits. They have
bodies divided into segments, jointed
legs, and a stiff exoskeleton. This is a
skeleton on the outside like a suit of
armor. But one way to tell if an animal is

an arachnid is to count its legs and body parts. While not every
adult arachnid has eight legs, most do. Arachnids also usually
have two main body parts. Centipedes belong to a group of
arthropods that have one pair of legs on each body segment.
And their bodies are made up of many segments—sometimes as
many as three hundred.

This book is about arachnids called
harvestmen. Harvestmen
are masters of defense.
They have many different—
sometimes even surprising—ways to
protect themselves from predators.

HARVESTMEN FACT

In some
parts of the world,
harvestmen are
nicknamed daddy
longlegs.

A harvestman's body
temperature rises and
falls with the temperature
around it. It must warm
up to be active.

HARVESTMEN ARE NOT SPIDERS

Harvestmen and spiders are both arachnids. Harvestmen even look a lot like spiders. But they're not spiders. Compare this spiny-headed harvestman to the European garden spider. Spiders have two clearly separate main body parts, the cephalothorax (sef-uh-loh-THOR-ax) and the abdomen. In harvestmen, these two parts are joined. Harvestmen appear to have one big, oval body. Some kinds of spiders are blind. Those with eyes, usually have eight. Some harvestmen are also blind, but those with eyes have just two. The eyes are on a bump on top of their heads.

Spiders are also known for their ability to spin silk. Harvestmen can't spin silk. They don't have any silk-producing glands.

HARVESTMEN FACT

Some harvestmen are active at night on snow-covered mountains and deep in underground caves.

SPINY-HEADED HARVESTMAN

EYES

CEPHALOTHORAX-ABDOMEN

ABDOMEN

CEPHALOTHORAX

EUROPEAN GARDEN SPIDER

Harvestmen also don't eat the way spiders do. Harvestmen, like this *Pantopsalis luna* (pan-TOP-sal-is LOO-nuh), eat solid bits of food. Spiders, like this wolf spider and most other kinds of arachnids, can only drink liquids. Their mouths are too tiny to take in anything bigger. The spider uses its digestive juices to break down its prey. Then it sucks in this liquid meal. The harvestman bites off small chunks of food and swallows them. The food is digested inside its body.

Spiders are known for producing venom (liquid poison) that they inject through fangs to kill their prey. Harvestmen lack fangs and don't produce venom. They grab their prey and hold onto it to eat it. Harvestmen also search for dead animals to feast on. Unlike spiders, they also sometimes eat rotting fruit or lap up plant juices.

HARVESTMEN FACT

It's a myth that harvestmen produce venom or become venomous by eating spiders.

PANTOPSALIS LUNA

BRAZILIAN WOLF SPIDER

OUTSIDE AND INSIDE

ON THE OUTSIDE

There are more than 6,400 different kinds of harvestmen. They all have their two main body parts—cephalothorax and abdomen—fused into one. Like all arachnids, their exoskeletons are made up of many plates. Tissues connect the plates so the harvestmen can bend and move. Take a look at this female *Mitopus morio* [mii-TOP-us MOR-ee-oh] harvestman to discover other features all harvestmen share.

LEGS:
Its four
pairs of legs
are used for walking,
climbing, hanging on,
and feeling. They may
also have sensors for
smell and taste.

CEPHALOTHORAX-ABDOMEN

EYES:
These detect light and send messages to the brain for sight.

CHELICERAE (KEH-liss-er-eye):
These jawlike parts in front of the mouth are edged with sharp teeth to crush prey and tear off bits.

PEDIPALPS:
These are a pair of leglike parts that extend from the head near the mouth. They help catch prey and hold it for eating.

SPIRACLES:
These holes help the harvestman breathe by letting air into and out of the body.

ON THE INSIDE

Look inside an adult female harvestman.

BRAIN:
The brain receives messages from body parts and sends signals back to them.

PHARYNX:
The muscles of this tube pull food into the digestive system.

ESOPHAGUS:
Food passes through this tube.

COXAL (KAHK-SEL) GLANDS:
These groups of cells collect liquid wastes and rid the body of them.

Approved by Dr. Simon Pollard,
Canterbury Museum,
Christchurch, New Zealand

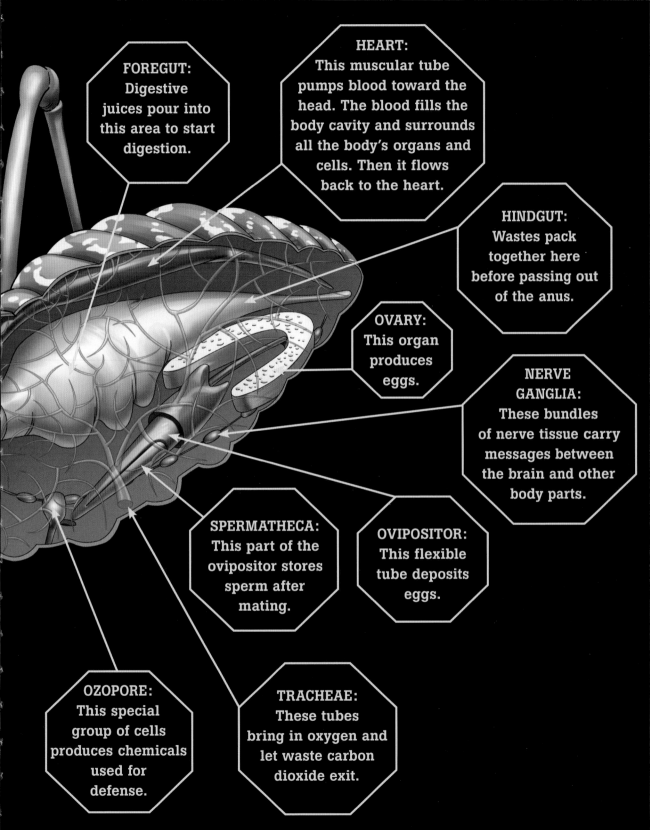

FOREGUT:
Digestive juices pour into this area to start digestion.

HEART:
This muscular tube pumps blood toward the head. The blood fills the body cavity and surrounds all the body's organs and cells. Then it flows back to the heart.

HINDGUT:
Wastes pack together here before passing out of the anus.

OVARY:
This organ produces eggs.

NERVE GANGLIA:
These bundles of nerve tissue carry messages between the brain and other body parts.

SPERMATHECA:
This part of the ovipositor stores sperm after mating.

OVIPOSITOR:
This flexible tube deposits eggs.

OZOPORE:
This special group of cells produces chemicals used for defense.

TRACHEAE:
These tubes bring in oxygen and let waste carbon dioxide exit.

BECOMING ADULTS

Like all arachnids, harvestmen become adults through incomplete metamorphosis (met-teh-MOR-feh-sus). *Metamorphosis* means "change." At the end of each stage, the harvestman sheds its exoskeleton and grows larger. A harvestman's life includes four stages: egg, larva, nymph, and adult. In some kinds of harvestmen, the nymph goes through several sub-stages of change, called instars, before it becomes an adult. Compare the *Santinezia serratotibialis* [san-tin-EEZ-ee-ah ser-RAH-toe-tib-ee-al-is] larvae with the adult. The young are similar to the adults, but they are smaller and can't reproduce.

SOME KINDS OF ARTHROPODS GO THROUGH COMPLETE METAMORPHOSIS. The four stages are egg, larva, pupa, and adult. Each stage looks and behaves very differently.

Some kinds of harvestmen that live where winters are cold pass the winter as eggs. They hatch and continue developing in the spring. Other kinds of harvestmen hatch and develop to the nymph stage. Then they pass the winter as nymphs and continue growing in the spring. Although some kinds of harvestmen take as long as three years to become adults, many have life cycles lasting just one year.

MOLTING TO GROW

When a harvestman grows bigger, it develops a new exoskeleton underneath the old one. Finally, the harvestman becomes so big its old exoskeleton is too tight. Most harvestmen get ready to molt, or shed, this old exoskeleton by hanging upside down from a leaf, a twig, or a bit of rock. Unlike spiders, which hang from a silk thread, harvestmen, like this *Phalangium opilio* (fah-LAN-gee-um oh-PIL-eh-oh), hold on with all four pairs of legs. Its exoskeleton splits open along the sides. Harvestmen tighten their bodies and stretch their legs to pull out of the old exoskeleton.

The new exoskeleton is soft at first. The harvestman forces blood into different parts of its body to stretch the soft exoskeleton. This way, like wearing clothes that are too big, the harvestman has room to grow before it has to molt again. It hides for a few hours after molting while the new exoskeleton hardens. After harvestmen become adults, they no longer molt.

FOR SELF-DEFENSE

The focus of a harvestman's life is staying safe and catching prey. Camouflage (blending in) is one feature that helps it do both. Check out how hard it is to spot this harvestman called *Iporangaia pustulosa* (ip-or-AN-gee-uh pus-tuu-LOH-suh) in its surroundings. Harvestmen are usually active at night when they are even harder to see.

Splay-legged harvestmen spread out their legs to help them hide in plain sight. Then they sit and wait to grab prey that comes close.

The second pair of the splay-legged harvestmen's legs is extra long. These help them feel their way when they travel.

Some kinds of harvestmen that live on the forest floor put on disguises. *Ortholasma* (or-thoh-LAZ-muh) has ridges on its back that form little pockets. These catch and hold grains of dirt to camouflage it. If that isn't enough to fool a predator, *Ortholasma* plays another trick. When it senses something big moving nearby, it pulls its legs in tight to its body. Then it keeps still and plays dead.

RIDGES ON BACK
(ENLARGED)

ORTHOLASMA WITH DIRT

Instead of keeping still, some long-legged harvestmen, like these *Leiobunum* (lie-oh-BUN-um), are likely to respond to danger by becoming superactive. They rapidly bob up and down. This works best when harvestmen are in a group. Bobbing together may make them appear to be a much larger animal—one that should be left alone.

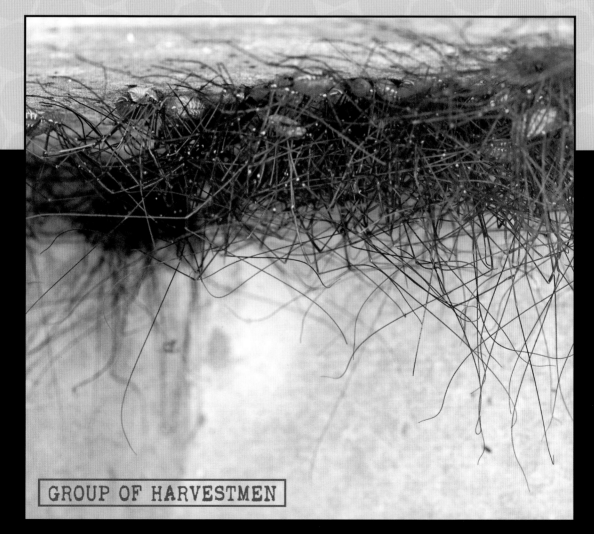

GROUP OF HARVESTMEN

Sometimes, though, a harvestman isn't able to escape being grabbed by a predator. That's why this Cosmetidae (koz–MEH–teh–dee) is missing one leg. Harvestmen are able to snap off a leg at the joint closest to the body. When that happens, a muscle pulls the joint into the body and seals the wound. That keeps the harvestman from bleeding. Meanwhile, the detached leg twitches. This happens because long-legged harvestmen have a pacemaker in each leg. A pacemaker's job is to send signals from the brain to the muscles that make the leg tip move. However, if a leg is snapped off, the pacemaker takes control of the leg. It continues sending signals to make the leg twitch—sometimes for as long as an hour. If the harvestman is lucky, the predator attacks the detached leg while the harvestman escapes. Unlike spiders, harvestmen are not able to regrow any lost body parts. Still, harvestmen can often live successfully even if they lose two or three legs.

ARMED WARFARE

Some harvestmen fight back if they are attacked. One kind, the *Geraeocormobius sylvarum* (jeh–ray–KOR–moh–bee–us sil–VAR–um) is armed with spiny legs *(below)*. When a predator grabs it, it folds its fourth pair of legs with a quick snap. That pinches whatever is caught between the two leg sections. This is usually enough to make the predator let go and back off.

Most harvestmen have another means of attacking to defend themselves—chemical warfare. Look at the orange blobs on *Serracutisoma* (ser-rah-KUU-teh-soh-muh) *(below)*. Those are droplets of chemicals it makes to defend itself. Harvestmen have a pair of special glands called ozopores to produce these chemicals.

This type of harvestman can release drops of the chemical through openings on each side of its body near the second pair of legs. Different kinds of harvestmen produce different chemicals. But all these chemicals cause the same result. Predators pause or back off, letting the harvestman escape.

DEFENSIVE CHEMICALS

Little, short-legged cyphopthalmids (sii-fop-THAL-midz) pick up chemical drops from their ozopores with the tips of their legs. Then they slap these on their attacker. Other kinds of harvestmen use their legs to spread droplets of the chemicals over their own bodies. The chemicals act as a predator repellent. A few kinds of harvestmen are able to squirt out a chemical spray. The spray shoots toward the harvestman's rear end. So when attacked, the harvestman turns its back on its enemy and fires.

Chemical warfare doesn't always work, though. A harvestman's ozopores can only store a small amount of the chemical. Once this is used up, it may take from a few days to a week for the harvestman to produce more. So some predators, like a bigger harvestman, may just keep on attacking. The little harvestman's chemical repelled its attacker at first. But when the chemical ran out, the bigger harvestman caught and ate its prey.

ALL FOR THE FAMILY

Some adult male and female harvestmen look very different from each other. Male harvestmen, like this wandering harvestman *(below)*, may be smaller and more colorful than the females. They are also more fiercely armed with spikes and spines and have larger chelicerae. When adult males have these kinds of features, they usually fight for mates. Or they use them to defend territories that have well-protected sites for hiding eggs.

HARVESTMEN FACT

In a few kinds of harvestmen, the males guard the eggs. Then the females fight one another for a mate.

After mating, many kinds of harvestmen females hide their eggs. Female harvestmen have a flexible, tubelike ovipositor. It can be extended from the female's body to deposit the eggs. Females with a long ovipositor deposit their eggs deep inside cracks and holes in the ground, in rocks, or in logs. There the eggs stay safe from predators and from drying out. Females that guard their eggs have a short ovipositor. *Santinezia serratotibialis* (san-tin-EEZ-ee-ah ser-RAH-toe-tib-ee-al-is) *(below)* will stand watch over her eggs for forty days until the larvae hatch. Then she'll remain with her young for about two more weeks until the larvae molt, becoming nymphs. When the nymphs leave the nest site, they're ready to find food and defend themselves.

DANGEROUS DAYS

It's summer in the southeastern United States. Dewdrops cling to blades of grass, and newly opened flowers glisten in the morning sun. Laughing and talking, a boy and a girl hurry from a house and across the grass. They don't notice the female *Leiobunum* [lie-oh-BUN-um] nymph drinking dew. Even if the children had looked in her direction, the harvestman would have been hard to spot. Her long legs are as thin as a human hair. Her body, about the size of an unpopped popcorn kernel, is close to the ground. Her plain brown coloring lets her blend in.

The children don't know the female harvestman is nearby, but she's aware of them. Sensors on her legs pick up the small movements in the air or on the ground from their footsteps. The harvestman's two eyes can only tell light from dark, but that's enough to let her know when the children pass by. The nymph keeps still to hide in plain sight. Even after her senses let her know the danger has passed, she remains still a few more minutes. Then she walks on. She has something important to do.

Like most harvestmen, this nymph is usually only active at night. She spends her days resting under leaves in the garden. There she's hidden from most predators, and her body is less likely to dry out. But this day, her armorlike exoskeleton is tight because she has grown so much. She climbs up a branch, holds on, and hangs upside down. She is ready to molt. When her old exoskeleton splits open, she pulls in her body to free it from the old skin. Then she tugs her legs and body out through the opening. Her body is already covered with a new bigger exoskeleton. It is soft at first, but once the new exoskeleton hardens, the harvestman nymph will have room to grow again.

HUNTING AGAIN

As the day's bright light fades, the harvestman nymph is ready to eat. She hunts for prey by sitting still and waiting. After a bit, when no prey comes close, the nymph walks on. With each step, her extra-long second pair of legs wave back and forth. Her legs are covered with sensory hairs so she explores as she goes. This way she finds a dead tiger beetle. She breaks open the beetle's hard exoskeleton with her chelicerae. Then she scoops bits of the soft tissue into her mouth.

Later, while she sits and waits again, an earthworm crawls close. Harvestmen don't pounce the way spiders do. She simply grabs her prey with her pedipalps and chelicerae. Without silk to wrap up her prey or venom to kill it, the harvestman holds on tight and takes a bite. She keeps on eating until she has her fill.

THE CYCLE CONTINUES

The female harvestman continues to eat and grow. By early autumn, she is ready to molt for the last time. This time, when she emerges from her old exoskeleton, she's an adult, able to reproduce. Much of her food energy will go into developing eggs inside her body. In time, her eggs are nearly half her body weight.

She gives off pheromones. These are special chemicals for communication. These signal she's a *Leiobunum* female ready to mate. Harvestmen only mate with their own kind. A male *Leiobunum* tracks her. He's only about one-third her size. When he finds her, he rubs her chelicerae and legs. She accepts this courtship and doesn't attack. The male transfers his sperm (male reproductive cells) into her body.

FEMALE

MALE

The male leaves to find more mates. The female goes hunting again. In a few days, she's ready to deposit her eggs. She searches for a crack in the ground. Then she pushes in her long ovipositor and deposits some eggs. She repeats this, hiding more than a hundred eggs in all. Because they are hidden, they'll survive through the winter.

OVIPOSITOR

In the spring, the young will hatch and go hunting, and the harvestmen's cycle of life continues.

HARVESTMEN AND OTHER TRICKY ARACHNIDS

HARVESTMEN belong to a group, or order, of arachnids called Opiliones (oh–PIL-ee-oh-neez). There are over 6,400 different kinds worldwide. They are found on all continents except Antarctica. Scientists group living and extinct animals with others that are similar. So harvestmen are classified this way:

> kingdom: Animalia
> phylum: Arthropoda
> class: Arachnida
> order: Opiliones

HELPFUL OR HARMFUL? Harvestmen are helpful because they eat insects. That helps control insect populations that might otherwise become pests. They also scavenge, eating dead plant and animal material, so they help clean up their habitat. In addition, harvestmen provide food for bigger predators, including other arachnids.

HOW BIG IS a *Leiobunum* harvestman? A female's head and body together are only about 0.27 inches (0.69 centimeters) long.

MORE ARACHNID DEFENDERS

Harvestmen have many varied ways to defend themselves. Check out ways other arachnids stay safe. How are these similar to the harvestmen's defenses? How are they different?

Giant vinegaroons have a long tail but lack a stinger. Instead, they spray a mist of vinegarlike acid from a gland at the base of their tail. While this isn't likely to kill a predator, such as a bird, it's irritating. That's usually enough to make the predator pull back. Found in tropical regions throughout the world, vinegaroons only spray as a last resort. They mainly stay safe by hunting their insect prey at night. Then their dark color lets them hide in plain sight.

Mexican red-knee tarantulas—like most tarantulas from North, Central, or South America—have their abdomens covered with barbed (spiked) hairs. When the tarantula is threatened by another predator, it turns its back on its enemy. Then it briskly rubs its hind legs against its abdomen. The barbed hairs are only loosely attached to the exoskeleton. Rubbing launches hairs, thousands of them, into the air. When the hairs strike, they irritate, itch, or hurt. If they strike an animal's eyes, they may cause temporary blindness. This defensive strike is usually enough to make the predator back off, giving the tarantula a chance to escape.

Hooded tick spiders have helmetlike hoods that can be raised and lowered to cover their heads. If the tick spider is attacked, this hood protects its mouth and chelicerae. A female also uses her hood to protect her developing young. Once the female deposits her eggs, she uses her legs to move them to her head under her hood. Hooded tick spiders are tiny, just 0.25 to 0.50 inches (0.6 to 1.3 cm) long. Carrying her eggs with her, a female keeps her brood safe from bigger predators while she hunts for even tinier prey.

GLOSSARY

abdomen: the back end of an arachnid where systems for digestion and reproduction are located. In harvestmen this is fused with the cephalothorax.

adult: the final stage of an arachnid's life cycle. Arachids are able to reproduce at this stage.

brain: the organ that receives messages from sense organs and other body parts and sends signals to control them

cephalothorax: the front end of an arachnid where the mouth, the brain, and the eyes, if any, are located. Legs are also attached to the cephalothorax. In harvestmen this is fused with the abdomen.

chelicerae: a pair of strong, jawlike parts in front of the mouth. In harvestmen they have a sawlike edge to crush and tear.

coxal glands: special groups of cells for collecting and getting rid of liquid wastes

egg: a female reproductive cell; the first stage of an arachnid's life cycle

esophagus: a tube through which food passes

exoskeleton: the protective, armorlike skeleton covering the outside of the body

eyes: sensory organs that detect light and send signals to the brain for sight

foregut: the place where digestive juices collect to start digestion

heart: a muscular tube that pumps blood throughout the body

hindgut: the place where water is absorbed and wastes are packed together before passing out of the anus

instar: a stage of change between molts

molt: the process of shedding an exoskeleton

nerve ganglia: bundles of nerve tissue that carry messages between the brain and other body parts

ovary: the body part that produces eggs

ovipositor: a flexible tube that can be extended outside the body to deposit eggs

ozopore: a group of cells that produces and gives off defensive chemicals

pedipalps: a pair of leglike body parts that extends from the head near the mouth. Pedipalps help catch prey and hold it for eating.

pharynx: a tube through which muscles pull food into the digestive system

pheromones: chemicals given off as a form of communication

sperm: a male reproductive cell

spermatheca: the part of the ovipositor in female harvestmen where sperm are stored after mating

spiracle: a small opening in the exoskeleton that leads into the tracheae

tracheae: tubes that let in air through openings, called spiracles. The tubes help spread oxygen throughout the spider's body. They also store oxygen.

DIGGING DEEPER

To keep on investigating harvestmen, explore these books and online sites.

BOOKS

Bishop, Nic. *Forest Explorer: A Life-Sized Field Guide*. New York: Scholastic, 2004. Explore the forest habitat and investigate the harvestmen's role in this habitat.

Heos, Bridget. *What to Expect When You're Expecting Larvae*. Minneapolis: Millbrook Press, 2011. Engaging text and colorful art help young readers understand the larva stage of development.

Stewart, Melissa. *A Daddy Longlegs Isn't a Spider*. Lakeville, MN: Windward Publishing, 2009. Discover true facts about how harvestmen live through this fictional story.

Townsend, John. *Incredible Arachnids*. Chicago: Heinemann–Raintree, 2005. See how harvestmen are like other arachnids and how they're different.

MORE FROM SANDRA MARKLE

INSECT WORLD:
Diving Beetles
Hornets
Locusts
Luna Moths
Mosquitoes
Praying Mantises
Stick Insects
Termites

WEBSITES

Amber Holds Arachnids Secret

http://news.bbc.co.uk/2/hi/science/nature/7327038.stm

Watch the video to find out about harvestmen that lived in ancient times. See a microscopic view of a harvestman trapped in amber.

The Harvestmen, or Grand-Daddy Longlegs, Is Not a Spider

http://www.hsu.edu/content.aspx?id=7439

Great close-up photos show why harvestmen aren't spiders. Also, discover how mites use harvestmen.

Hug a Bug

http://www.bugs.org/Activities/Activity_M-10%20hugabug.pdf

This site shows the steps to follow to observe a harvestman. Share this activity with an adult partner.

University of Michigan— BioKids

http://www.biokids.umich.edu/critters/Opiliones/

This site answers questions about the life and habits of harvestmen.

LERNER 🅔 SOURCE™

Visit www.lerneresource.com for free, downloadable arachnid diagrams, research assignments to use with this series, and additional information about arachnid scientific names.

HARVESTMEN ACTIVITY

Harvestmen are believed to have very poor vision. They are probably only able to tell light from dark. Long-legged harvestmen use one of their pairs of legs as antennae. Follow these steps to get a feel for how a long-legged harvestman investigates its world.

1. Collect clear tape and six plastic drinking straws—the kind with a bendable hinge. Have an adult partner help you tape three straws together to make one long straw. Repeat to make a second long straw. Bend these slightly at each hinge. These are like a long-legged harvestman's segmented legs.

2. Work in an open area of a room. Help your adult partner arrange stacks of pillows or piles of blankets and towels to create three obstacles in a row. Hold one long straw leg in each hand. Stretch these out to extend your reach well beyond your body. Have your partner use a scarf to blindfold you.

3. Have your partner guide you to the first obstacle. Your partner will walk with you to be sure you don't get off course, but you will need to find your way around the obstacles. Move your straw legs back and forth to find and go around each obstacle.

Now check out the following website to watch a long-legged harvestman finding its way through the world: http://www.kidport.com/RefLIB/Science/Videos/Animals/Arachnids/Harvestmen.htm.

INDEX

PHOTO ACKNOWLEDGMENTS

The images in this book are used with the permission of: © James Robinson/Animals Animals, p. 4; © Ken Preston-Mafham/Premaphotos, pp. 5, 24; © Stefan Sollfors/Science Faction/CORBIS, p. 7 (bottom); © Alex Hyde/Minden Pictures, p. 7 (top); © Dr. Simon D. Pollard, p. 9 (top); © João Burini, p. 9 (bottom); © Joe Warfel/Eighth-Eye Photography, pp. 10-11, 15, 18, 21, 22-23, 25, 26, 27, 28, 29, 30-31, 32-33, 34, 35, 36-37, 38, 39; © Bill Hauser/Independent Picture Service, pp. 12-13; © Bryan E. Reynolds, p. 17; © Premaphotos/NPL/Minden Pictures, p. 19; © Dr. William A. Shear, p. 20 (top); © Marshal Hedin, pp. 20 (bottom), 46-47; © Daniel Heuclin/NHPA/Photoshot, p. 41 (top); © Mark Bowler/NHPA/Photoshot, p. 41 (center); © Piotr Naskrecki/NHPA/Photoshot, p. 41 (bottom).

Front cover: © Premaphotos/NPL/Minden Pictures.